MINISTERING ANGELS OF GOD

WHO ARE ON ASSIGNMENT FROM THE CREATOR

Author: Marie Lake

Marie Lake

Lambeth

London

England

Paulanthony Skerrett - Cover Design

Unless otherwise indicated, all scriptures quotations are taken from the King James Version of the Bible.

DEDICATION

I am dedicating this book to my great grandson Rowan Jones who was gone before he entered the world.

I know he is definitely with our Saviour the Almighty GOD.

ABOUT THE AUTHOR

Marie Lake is a mother, grandmother, and great grandmother.

She loves reading, praying and offering her time volunteering for the work of the LORD, in the church.

Marie Lake also likes to encourage others and loves looking after her grandchildren.

TABLE OF CONTENTS

Angels Minister

Angels Seen Mostly in White Apparel

Angels Do Eat

Scripture Tells Us Our Words Are Recorded

Angels Deliver Us

The Angel of the LORD went to Gideon

For He is called the Prince of Peace

The Angel of the LORD foretold the birth of Samson

Angels Bring Answer to Prayers

The Arch Angel Gabriel brings Joy

Shepherd's first told of the coming of Christ

Angels rolled away the stone

Angels to give instruction

Satan Counterfeits GOD

My Testimony

One of my favourite songs

The Angel of the LORD opens up prison doors

Phillip commissioned by the angel of the LORD

The Angel of the LORD stands by His people

FOREWORD

The presence of angels in everyday life may easily be overlooked in a world where we do not place our minds on such things. We have been generally educated to see random luck or coincidences as affecting our lives rather than divine intervention. The purpose of this book is to remind all GOD's people that angels have always impacted and continue to impact on human existence. Many examples of angelic interventions in everyday life are found in scriptures and such examples provide poignant lessons.

A multitude of angels reside in heaven and move amongst us on earth with the purpose of doing the bidding of the Most High GOD. Angels are not to be worshipped. The main categories of angels which appear in the bible are the seraphim who are mainly seen to worship the creator, the cherubim who generally guard sacred things, and the archangels such as Gabriel, who appear as messengers and warriors, as is the case with Michael the archangel. These archangels and angels may be sent to give messages to us and may also be sent to defend us from evil.

Over all, there is the Angel of the LORD.

Makeda Sapia

Angels were sent to guard the tree of life

Angels were first mentioned in the bible in the book of Genesis when Adam and Eve sinned. They were cast out of the beautiful garden of Eden; in this garden was the tree of life, which GOD did not want them to eat from.

If they had eaten from the tree of life after they sinned, they would have become immortal beings who could never die, but would be plagued with sickness, disease, and all the negative things of this world, never to be rid of them.

This is why GOD had to put them out of the garden, and placed angels at the entrance of the garden, to guard the tree of life.

GENESIS 3 : 24

3 So He drove out the man; and He placed cherubims at the east of the garden of Eden, and a flaming sword which turned every way, to keep the way of the tree of life.

The Bible tells us that there are angelic beings called cherubims and seraphims but let us look further into this as some people say that these beings have wings while others say that they do not possess wings.

ISAIAH 6 : 1 - 7

1 In the year that King Uzziah died, I saw also the LORD sitting upon a throne, high and lifted up, and His train filled the temple.

2 Above it stood the seraphims: each one had six wings with twain he covered his face, and with twain he covered his feet, and with twain he did fly.

3 And one cried unto another, and said, Holy,
holy, holy, the whole earth is full of his glory.

4 And the posts of the door moved at the voice of
him that cried, and the house was filled with
smoke.

5 Then said I, woe is me! I am undone; because I
am a man of unclean lips, and I dwell in the midst
of a people of unclean lips: for mine eyes have
seen the King, the LORD of hosts.

6 Then flew one of the seraphims unto me, having
a live coal in his hand, which he had taken with
the tongs from off the altar:

7 And he laid it upon my mouth, and said, Lo, this
hath touched thy lips; and thine iniquity is taken
away, and thy sin is purged.

By contemplating on these verses, you will be able to decide for yourselves what scripture tells us about these beings. What do you think?

I believe it depends on who the angel is, as we must remember they mostly appear on earth in human form. Hebrews 13:2 says "Be not forgetful to entertain strangers: for thereby some have entertained angels unawares." This means that in the natural realm we may not see any wings, but we must also note that the wings can be invisible, as all angels can appear and disappear at will.

There are different categories of angelic forces and they have different roles. They can also take on different features depending on whether they are good angels or bad angels.

When an angel appears to an individual, they come so unexpectedly and may present a frightening experience. For example, Zachariah who was at the altar burning incense was not expecting to see anyone near the Holy of Holies (Luke 1:11-12). Mary the mother of Jesus, who was in a room by herself and so many other people had similar frightening experiences (Luke 1:28-30). You will find that the first words that come from an angel's mouth is usually, “Do not be afraid.” Just imagine you are in a place by yourself, you know for certain no other person is there beside you, and then you have a sudden appearance and you hear the words “Do not be afraid”. How do you think you would feel?

When you read the description Ezekiel gave of the angelic beings he saw, it makes one wonder how terrible looking they are. These angels have eyes everywhere all over their bodies.

EZEKIEL 10 : 14

14 And every one had four faces: the first face was the face of a cherub, and the second face was the face of a man, and the third face of a lion, and the fourth face of an eagle.

EZEKIEL 10 : 21

21 Everyone had four faces apiece, and every one four wings; and the likeness of the hands of a man was under their wings.

Many people either buy or they make a statue or sculpture of a cherub, which is usually like a small person with wings. There are many different statues of angels and cherubs all over the world of varying sizes. A lot of these statues are often found in churches.

Angel of the Lord Intervenes

GENESIS 16 : 7 - 10

Hagar was an Egyptian, she was also Sarai's maid and a second wife to Abraham. Hagar had left home with her child Ishmael, Abraham's first child, as she had been receiving harsh treatment from Sarai, who had not yet been able to bear a child for Abraham and was hurting.

During this difficult time with her mistress, Hagar left home and had an encounter with the angel of the LORD. The angel advised her to return to her mistress, and she was obedient to the angel which was our LORD.

(If you read my book on The Angel of the LORD, you will receive more information on this subject and also have a better understanding).

GENESIS 21 : 12 – 21

12 And GOD said unto Abraham, Let it not be grievous in thy sight because of the lad, and because of thy bondwoman; in all that Sarah hath said unto thee, hearken unto her voice; for in Isaac shall thy seed be called.

13 And also of the son of the bondwoman will I make a nation, because he is thy seed.

14 And Abraham rose up early in the morning, and took bread, and a bottle of water, and gave it unto Hagar, putting it on her shoulder, and the child, and sent her away: and she departed, and wandered in the wilderness of Beersheba.

15 And the water was spent in the bottle, and she cast the child under one of the shrubs.

16 And she went, and sat her down over against him a good way off, as it was bowshot: for she said, Let me not see the death of the child. And she went, and sat over against him, and left up her voice, and wept.

17 And GOD heard the voice of the lad; and the
angel of GOD called to Hagar out of heaven, and
said unto her, What aileth thee, Hagar? Fear not;
for GOD has heard the voice of the lad where he
is.

18 Arise, lift up the lad, and hold him in thine
hand; for I will make him a great nation.

19 And GOD opened her eyes, and she saw a well
of water; and she went, and filled the bottle with
water, and gave the lad drink.

20 And GOD was with the lad; and he grew, and
dwelt in the wilderness, and became an archer

21 And he dwelt in the wilderness of Paran: and
his mother took him a wife out of the land of
Egypt.

Hagar had to finally leave Sarai, her mistress and set out on her journey. Hagar and her son Ishmael, travelled through the desert and when they had consumed all the water they had, her son was parched and it seemed like he would not make it. Hagar could not watch him die, so she went a distance away from him and waited for him to go.

In this instance, the angel of the LORD did not appear to her in the same way he had done when he first visited her. This time He called her from out of heaven. He instructed her to go to her son and hold him, which she did; like the first occasion when He prophesied into her life and named her child Ismael. However, this time Hagar's eyes were then opened to see a spring.

Notice that her eyes were not opened to see the well until she had obeyed Him by lifting up the lad and holding him in her hands. Things can happen supernaturally when we trust in GOD and obey Him.

Oh, what a Saviour mighty to save! No matter what life throws at us, He is able to do things that seem impossible. He rescues us in a way only He can. Who else can we depend upon? No one else but Jesus!

Abraham had a similar experience when he was about to offer up Isaac as a burnt offering unto the LORD and again the angel of the LORD called out from heaven in the same way He did to Hagar when she had given up hope.

GENESIS 22 : 11 - 22

11 And the angel of the LORD called unto him out of heaven, and said, Abraham, Abraham: and he said, Here am I.

12 And he said, Lay not thine hand upon the lad, neither do thou anything unto him: for now I know that thou fearest GOD, seeing that thou hast not withheld thy son, thine only son from me.

In this scenario we see Abraham doing the opposite of what he had intended because he had faith in the GOD he served. How many of us can say, if we were in that circumstance that we would have done the same as Abraham?

When Moses was to deliver the children of Israel out of bondage, he was told by GOD that after everything that was said and done Pharaoh's heart would be hardened. Pharaoh did not want to release the children of GOD, and GOD had to go to the extreme and send a death angel to remove the Egyptians first born.

You might think this was too harsh. But you need to remember GOD is a righteous Judge. This only happened because Pharaoh had killed the children that were born to the Israelites for eighty years, causing the infant sons to be thrown in the river.

We need to repent of our sins and not think GOD will let us get away with what we do to each other.

Once we repent He wipes the slate clean. Thank you Jesus.

He saved the Israelites first born by having them put the blood of a lamb over their lintels and doorposts. This represents the shed blood of Jesus. It was a foreshadow of things to come. GOD looks at us through the blood of Jesus and does not see our sins. Amen.

Guidance of the Israelites Angel

EXODUS 23 : 20 – 23

20 Behold, I send an Angel before thee, to keep thee in the way, and to bring thee into the place which I have prepared.

21 Beware of him, and obey his voice, provoke him not; for he will not pardon your transgressions: for my name is in him.

22 But if thou shalt indeed obey his voice, and do all that I speak; then I will be an enemy unto thine enemies, and an adversary unto thine adversaries.

23 For mine Angel shall go before thee, and bring thee in unto the Amorites, and the Hittites, and the Perizzites, and the Canaanites, the Hivites, and the Jebusites: and I will cut them off.

The Angel of the LORD always guides GOD's people. He makes sure that we walk in the way GOD has planned for us and that we do not go astray but grow from strength to strength in His power and might.

GOD wanted the Israelites to be aware of the Angel. He wanted them to do what is right and to follow what He told them to do. They were not to upset him by not walking in his way or listening to the instructions he gives them.

They were also warned that He would not pardon them. There is only one who can pardon sins and that is GOD, so we thank GOD for His son Jesus who always forgives us each time we fall and ensures that the door of mercy is still kept ajar for us. The promise GOD made to the Israelites that He will be an enemy to our enemies and an adversary to our adversary is available to us today.

You need to know that GOD is able to put our enemies to flight, but not only can He do that, He can make our enemies become our friends. Thank GOD.

Joshua Angel Encounter

Joshua was a real man of GOD who was always on the LORD's side. The angel of the LORD made a visitation to him and in doing so the GOD of heaven allows Joshua and his people to know that the King is in our midst, and we have nothing to fear. When the LORD is with us, we just want to give Him the praise due to His matchless name. When Joshua gave Him worship, He told him to remove his shoes from off his foot, for where Joshua was standing was holy ground. He also told Moses the same words.

JOSHUA 5 : 15

15 And the captain of the LORD'S host said unto Joshua, Loose thy shoe from off thy foot; for the place whereon thou standest is holy. And Joshua did so."

When Moses had his encounter, he wanted to take a closer look when he was called and told where he stood as holy ground.

EXODUS 3 : 5

5 And he said, draw not nigh hither: put off thy shoes from off thy feet, for the place whereon thou standest is holy ground.

Jacob Surrounded by Angels

GENESIS 32 : 1 - 2

1 And Jacob went on his way, and the angels of GOD met him.

2 And when Jacob saw them, he said, this is GOD's host: and he called the name of that place Mahanaim.

The word 'Mahaniam' means 'two companies' though he said GOD's host using a singular term, he named the place 'Mahanaim' for the angels. The angels then divided themselves one group at the front and one group at the back. This event 'Mahaniam' took place after Jacob had left his uncle and his brethren behind after they chased him and his family for leaving.

After many years, Jacob met his brother Esau and his four hundred men. This was his first time going back home, after fleeing from his brother because he had taken both his birthright and blessings.

The company of angels ordered themselves; one group at the front and one group at the back to give Jacob comfort in knowing that the LORD was with him. This encourages us to be aware that we have angels as our guide. According to one's assignment in life we are given the appropriate amount of angels that we need. Know that GOD will always protect us. He will be with us wherever we go. Even if we do not see His angels, both He and His angels are with us.

Angels Do Not Marry or Procreate

MATTHEW 22 : 30

30 But are as the angels in heaven

In this chapter, the Sadducees who did not believe in the resurrection questioned the Master about what Moses had told the children of Israel. Moses had told them if they married and the husband died before having children that if the deceased had a brother, the brother should marry his brother's widow. The first child from this marriage should be considered that of the dead brother.

They were saying to Jesus - Yeshua, what if they were seven brothers and they all married this woman and there was no child? Whose wife would she be after they all had died? Jesus told them they shall be like the angels of GOD because there is no marriage in heaven. After we have passed from this world, we will have an idea how the angels feel since we will be equal to them.

Disobedient Angels

An example of angels not obeying the order of GOD can be seen in the incident that happened in Genesis 6 when GOD chained them up because they had broken the rules of GOD.

GENESIS 6 : 1 - 8

1 And it came to pass, when men began to multiply on the face of the earth, and daughters were born unto them

2 That the sons of GOD saw the daughters of men that they were fair; and they took them wives of all which they chose.

3 And the LORD said, My spirit shall not always strive with man, for that he also is flesh: yet his days shall be an hundred and twenty years.

4 There were giants in the earth in those days; and also after that, when the sons of GOD in unto the daughters of men, and they bare children to them,

the same became mighty men and were of old, men of renown.

5 And GOD saw that the wickedness of man was great in the earth, and that every imagination of the thoughts of his heart was only evil continually.

6 And it repented the LORD that he had made man on the earth, and it grieved him at his heart.

7 And the LORD said, I will destroy man whom I have created from the face of the earth; both man and beast, and the creeping thing, and the fowls of the air; for it repenteth me that I have made them.

8 But Noah found grace in the eyes of the LORD.

You have read that they came to earth and had sexual relationships with human beings, and when they did this they produced a race called Nephilim. The Nephilim people were giants, good fighters and also great hunters. This incident caused GOD to be angry with them and pronounce a punishment on them.

In addition, angels cannot die; they are immortal beings as we see in the second book of Peter .

2ND PETER 2 : 4

4 For if GOD spared not the angels that sinned, but cast them down to hell, and delivered them into chains of darkness, to be reserved unto judgement.

JUDE 1 : 6

6 And the angels that kept not their first estate, but left their own habitation, he hath reserved in everlasting chains under darkness unto the judgement of the great day.

GOD has Appointed Angels for Children

ST. MATTHEW 18 : 10

10 Take heed that ye despite not one of these little ones; for I say unto you, That in heaven their angels do always behold the face of my Father which is in heaven.

Jesus teaches us that we must be aware of what we do to children, because they are assigned guardian angels and these angels see our Father face daily, so if anyone does evil to a child and does not repent it, it will not be in their best interest.

Little children are precious in the sight of GOD and I believe this is because they are innocent. You will also find in scripture that Jesus wants us to be as little children not holding malice and such negative attitudes in us, so that we can enter into the kingdom of GOD. Furthermore, children are so trusting; for example if they are crossing a busy road with their parents, you will see they are not afraid, they trust that no harm will befall them. Jesus wants the same childlike trusting with us his people.

Angels Usher our Spirit into the Presence of the LORD

LUKE 16 : 19 - 22

19 There was a certain man rich man, which was clothed in purple and fine linen , and fared sumptuously every day:

20 And there was a certain beggar named Lazarus, which was laid at his gate, full of sores,

21 And desiring to be fed with the crumbs which fell from the rich man's table: moreover the dogs came and licked this sores.

22 And it came to pass, that the beggar died, and was carried by angels into Abraham's bosom.

Look at verse 22 closely and notice that when a man dies he does not cross over alone - Angels usher him to whatever place is his destination.

Let us accept Christ Jesus as our Saviour so that when it is time for us to leave this world, if the rapture has not occurred by then we will be with our LORD. There are angels that GOD has given an assignment to watch over us and they are always with us every step of the way. They guide and protect us.

Furthermore, our angels are also able to call for assistance in a moment to assist them when they are in difficulty. Just as what you have read in Daniel when his angel was held up by the Prince of Persia and Michael came to his rescue.

However, the fallen angels do all in their power to sabotage GODs plan for our lives. Who are fallen angels? These are the angels that were led by the devil to rebel and attempted a mutiny against GOD.

Everlasting Fire for the Devil and his Angels

ST. MATTHEW 25 : 41

41 Then shall he say also unto them on the left hand, Depart from me, ye cursed, into everlasting fire, prepared for the devil and his angels.

Now these are the ones that rebelled against GOD. You can see it is a person's doing that will take them to hell, for hell was not made for us. It was made for the devil and his angels. I pray that mankind grasp the truth of this truth and accept Jesus as LORD and Saviour before it is too late.

HEBREWS 9 : 27

27 And as it is appointed unto men once to die, but after this comes the judgement.

Satan and Angels Revolt GOD

When Satan wanted to take over from GOD he convinced one third of the angels to attempt to overthrow the throne of GOD, our GOD did not lift a finger. He simply got angel Michael to deal with Satan and his cohorts.

REVELATIONS 12 : 7 – 9

7 And there was war in heaven: Michael and his angels fought against the dragon; and the dragon fought and his angels.

8 And prevailed not; neither was their place found any more in heaven.

9 And the great dragon was cast out, that old serpent, called the Devil which deceiveth the whole world: he was cast out into the earth, and his angels were cast out with him.

ISAIAH 14 : 12 – 15 further provides more information about this;

12 How are thou fallen from heaven, O Lucifer,
son of the morning! How art thou cut down to the
ground, which didst weaken the nations!

13 For thou hast said in thine heart, I will ascend
into heaven, I will exalt my throne above the stars
of GOD: I will sit also upon the mount of the
congregation, in the sides of the north;

14 I will ascend above the heights of the clouds; I
will be like the Most High.

15 Yet thou shalt be brought down to hell, to the
sides of the pit.

The reader can also refer to Ezekiel 28 : 12 - 19 for more information on this.

Deformities and paralysis may not be of natural causes and what we think it is, it could be that some fallen angels have attached themselves to us. An example of this is when Jesus had to cast out the spirit of infirmity out of the woman.

ST. LUKE 13 : 11 – 13

11 And behold, there was a woman which had a spirit of infirmity eighteen years, and was bowed together, and could not in no wise lift up herself.

12 And when Jesus saw her, he called her to him, and said unto her, Woman, thou art loosed from thine infirmity.

13 And he laid hands on her: and immediately she was made straight, and glorified GOD.

Jesus Witnesses Satan Falling

ST. LUKE 10 : 18

18 And he said unto them, I beheld Satan as lightning fall from heaven.

This is information that you know is correct, Jesus does not hide anything that He knows from us. That is why we can trust in Him and believe His words, that He is gone to prepare a place for us and that He is coming back again.

We really need to be more vigilant watching, praying and praising GOD. When we sing praises we strengthen our angels and if our eyes were to open to the supernatural realm, you would see the angels in actual warfare on our behalf.

Angels That Fight On Our Behalf Are More Than Those That Fight Against Us

2ND KINGS 6 : 15 - 19

15 And when the servant of the man of GOD was risen early, and gone forth, behold, an host compassed the city both with horses and chariots. And his servant said unto him, Alas, my master! What shall we do?

16 And he answered, Fear not: for they that be with us are more than they that be with them.

17 And Elisha prayed, and said, LORD, I pray thee, open his eyes, that he may see. And the LORD opened the eyes of the young man; and he saw: and behold, the mountain was full of horses and chariots of fire round about Elisha.

These verses are self-explanatory, I could not put it any better way, and what you need to know is that the GOD who did this for Elisha has done it time and time again for us.

Only believe and when you find this difficult, be like the man who brought his son to the disciples and they could not heal him. When Jesus came down from the mountain the man told Him everything. He knew he did not really believe that his child could be healed so he cried out "help thou my unbelief".

The Master was pleased with that confession and the man's son was healed. The angels of GOD are always ministering to our needs whatever they may be.

PSALM 148 : 6

6 It says He hath also established them forever and ever.

Angels Rejoice

We should note that angels have emotions and this is proven when they rejoice over GOD's creation of the universe.

JOB 38 : 4 – 7

4 Where wast thou when I laid the foundations of the earth? declare, if thou hast understanding.

5 Who hath laid the measures thereof, if thou knowest? or who hath stretched the line upon it.

6 Where upon are the foundations thereof fastened? or who laid the corner stone thereof;

7 When the morning stars sang together, and all the sons of GOD shouted for joy?

Here we see they were created before the world was created. They like to rejoice so when the saints are praising the Most High they too are rejoicing.

LUKE 15 : 10

10 There is joy in the presence of the angels of GOD over one sinner that repenteth.

I believe that when we accept Jesus as our LORD and Saviour, angels are happy that He has not died in vain. For they witnessed everything from the time He came to earth until He returned to heaven.

Angels Minister

MARK 1 : 13

13 And he was there in the wilderness forty days, tempted of Satan; and was with the wild beasts; and the angels ministered unto him.

Here you see Christ being ministered to by the angels. We do not know how many they were but they were there for Him. They had to protect Him from the wild beasts that were in the wilderness and from being without food and water.

Likewise, GOD protects all His children by sending His angels to protect us from dangers seen or unseen. Children of GOD, please note some of us might be called by GOD to places we would rather not go to. However, be confident and know that the angels of GOD will protect you and minister to your needs even in those places.

LUKE 22 : 43

43 And there appeared an angel unto him from heaven, strengthening him.

When Jesus - Yeshua Hamashiach was in the garden of Gethsemane, all the sins of the world were placed upon Him and this caused Him to be in tremendous agony. At that moment in time, GOD sent an angel to strengthen Him.

Jesus knows all our every care and what seems impossible to man is always possible to GOD. Because He came in human form, He knows all that we go through because He has been through greater than us.

JOHN 16 : 33

33 In the world he shall have tribulation: but be of good cheer; I have overcome the world.

He has overcome the world and since we belong to Him, we too are overcomers through Him who loves us. He gave His life as a ransom for us. It does not matter what you are going through just keep holding on, you might be thinking I can't make it or I can't take it anymore, but just hold on in there, you will come through. There is light at the end of the tunnel. It does not matter how dark it may seem, Yeshua is right by your side and you will have reason to testify.

Angels Seen Mostly in White Apparel

JOHN 20 : 12

12 And seeth two angels in white sitting, the one at the head, and the other at the feet, where the body of Jesus had lain.

ACTS 1 : 9 - 11

9 And when he had spoken these things, while they beheld, he was taken up; and a cloud received him out of their sight.

10 And while they looked steadfastly toward heaven as he went up, behold two men stood by them in white apparel;

11 Which also said, Ye men of Galilee, why stand ye gazing up into heaven? this same Jesus, which is taken from you into heaven, shall so come in like manner as ye seen him go into heaven.

Angels Do Eat

PSALM 78 : 25

25 Man did eat angels' food.

The children of Israel were given manna from heaven when they came out of the land of Egypt, where they had been in bondage for four hundred years. GOD sent a deliverer whose name was Moses to deliver them.

As Moses led the children of Israel on the journey out of Egypt towards the promised land, they became hungry in the wilderness and GOD provided for His people. That is the beauty of GOD, He always provides for His children's needs. Glory to GOD.

Scripture Tells Us Our Words Are Recorded

ECCLESIASTES 5 : 6

6 Suffer not thy mouth to cause thy flesh to sin; neither say thou before the angel, that it was an error: wherefore should GOD be angry at thy voice.

The writer is King Solomon, a great king only surpassed by Christ Jesus because he was gifted in wisdom, knowledge and understanding, and GOD had revealed many things to him.

Here he is warning us that everything we say is recorded. GOD does not compel us to make vows to Him, so if we should do this we must honour it. Therefore, we need to be wise in what we say and think carefully before we speak.

When we break our vows to GOD, hearing our voice may cause Him to be angry with us and He may consider us as His ungrateful child. May He continue to have mercy on us. Amen.

Angels Deliver Us

GENESIS 19 : 15 - 16

15 And when the morning arose, then the angels hastened Lot saying, Arise, take thy wife, and thy two daughters, which are here; lest thou be consumed in the iniquity of the city.

16 And while he lingered the men laid hold of his hand, and upon his wife, and upon the hands of his two daughters; the being merciful unto him: and they brought him forth, and set him without the city.

Lot and his family were delivered from Sodom when angels were sent to deliver him and his family. GOD was merciful unto him because Lot did not sin against GOD by doing what those men were doing amongst themselves. Likewise, GOD is always delivering us from danger seen or unseen.

There is no need for us to worry about anything, we should just live each day trusting in Jesus and all shall be well with us.

The Angel of the LORD went to Gideon

When the Children of Israel were going through trying times after they had been disobedient to GOD and He had delivered them into the hands of the Midianites, they cried out to GOD when they could not take the oppression anymore and GOD heard their cry.

The angel of the LORD went to Gideon for he was going to deliver God's people through him. When he went to Gideon and conversed with him, Gideon asked him to wait to receive a present from his hands. The angel said he would wait. Gideon went and prepared the food items for him. When Gideon presented the meal to him, he told Gideon how to place it on the altar.

JUDGES 6 : 21 - 24

21 Then the angel of the LORD put forth the end of the staff that was in his hand, and touched the flesh and the unleavened cakes; and there rose up fire out of the rock, and consumed the flesh and the unleavened cakes, Then the angel of the LORD departed out of his sight.

22 and when Gideon perceived that he was an angel of the LORD, Gideon said, Alas, O LORD GOD! for because I have seen an angel of the LORD face to face.

23 And the LORD said unto him, Peace be unto thee; fear not: thou shalt not die.

24 Then Gideon built an altar there unto the LORD, and called it Jehovah-shalom

Here is a young man that GOD used to deliver His people. He knew that He could trust His son Gideon, the SON of GOD the second in the Trinity left His home in glory to encourage this Man of GOD so that together they would deliver the Children of Israel.

When Gideon realised that he had actually seen the LORD, he was afraid and he thought that he would die but our Saviour reassured him that he would not die. I am sure Gideon was very relieved which is why he made an altar and called it GOD of Peace.

For He is called the Prince of Peace

ISAIAH 9 : 6

6 And his name shall be called Wonderful, Counsellor, The mighty GOD, The everlasting Father and The Prince Of Peace.

Know that not only will He deliver us His people, but He will give us peace. A peace that the world cannot give to us because they cannot even comprehend it. It is a peace that passes all human understanding.

PHILIPPIANS 4 : 7

7 And the peace of GOD, which passeth all understanding, shall keep your hearts and mind through Christ Jesus.

The Angel of the LORD foretold the birth of Samson

GOD spoke to a barren woman that she would bear a son, that he would be a Nazarite unto the LORD and that he would deliver His people Israel GOD'S chosen people.

When the angel of the LORD left her, she told her husband Manoah everything and he wanted to see for himself. He prayed to the LORD to send the Man of GOD who his wife saw to come to him as well.

The angel of the LORD revealed himself again to the woman and she ran and called her husband. So He told the man everything that He had told the woman she should do.

He repeated Himself again for the man's benefit since He had requested it of him. Manoah wanted to detain Him until he and his wife had prepared a kid (young goat) for Him.

He plainly told Manoah that He would not detain Him neither would He eat bread from him. But if he would offer a burnt sacrifice he must do it unto the LORD.

JUDGES 13 : 19 - 23

19 So Manoah took a kid with a meat offering, and offered it upon a rock unto the LORD: and the angel did wondrously; and Manoah and his wife looked on.

20 For it came to pass, when the flame went towards heaven from off the altar, that the angel of the LORD ascended in the flame of the altar. And Manoah and his wife looked on it, and fell on their faces to the ground.

21 But the angel of the LORD did no more appear unto Manoah and his wife. Then Manoah knew he was an angel of the LORD.

Look at how GOD is preparing His son Samson to deliver His people Israel ahead of time. This should boost our confidence that GOD who sees everything from the beginning to end will always be our deliverer. He knows our comings and goings and he has put everything in order for His glory. All we need to do is to walk in His way and do what He has instructed us to do and victory shall be ours.

PSALM 91 : 11 – 12

11 For he shall give his angels charge over thee, to keep thee in all thy ways.

12 They shall bear thee up in their hands, lest thou dash thy feet against a stone.

The prophet Daniel was rescued by the angel of the LORD when he was cast into the lion's den.

PSALM 34: v 7

7 The angel of the LORD encampeth round about them that fear him, and delivereth them.

Praise GOD not only does He encamp around His people who love and revere Him, He also delivers them. How many times you may ask? The answer is twenty four times seven. How you may say? Answer. Because He is a Spirit.

Angels Bring Answer to Prayers

Also Daniel saw a vision of the Angel Gabriel who came to bring the answer to his prayer. Gabriel told him that his prayers were answered from the first day he prayed and that he had been held up by the prince of Persia until Michael came to rescue him so that he could freely deliver the message.

Daniel 10 : 12 - 13

12 Then said he unto me, Fear not, Daniel: for from the first day that thou didst set thy heart to understand, and to chasten thyself before GOD, thy words were heard, and I am come for thy words.

13 But the prince of the kingdom of Persia withstood me one and twenty days: but, lo,

Michael, one of the chief princes, came to help me: and I remained there with the kings of Persia.

So we see that angels are always doing the work of GOD. They are His messengers and we see that they can fight, but some can fight more than others.

Michael can fight more than Gabriel for he is a warrior, while Gabriel brings Joy. This shows us that GOD sends His angels to always fight for us and that when we pray, even if our answer does not come on time, we can be confident that it is on the way.

Keep on praying and after a while you can even begin to thank the Almighty in advance for what you were asking Him for. Knowing that it will be according to your faith.

The Arch Angel Gabriel brings Joy

ST. LUKE 1 : 11- 20

Angel Gabriel visited Zachariah when he was ministering in the priest's office; burning incense in the temple of the LORD and the people were outside praying. The angel told him that his prayer was answered and that his wife would give him a son.

Now because he and Elizabeth were old, he wanted the angel to give a sign as he did not believe. The angel caused him to be dumb and when he had finished ministering in the temple, he went home and exactly what Gabriel had told him came to pass. His wife conceived and brought forth a boy and at the baby's naming ceremony he received his voice back.

We find that the angel Gabriel visited Joseph in a dream and told him to marry Mary, for she was engaged to him and was found pregnant. The custom in those days was to stone the person found pregnant without being married. Joseph was a good man who did not want to do this to Mary and he was thinking of putting her away privately.

ST. MATTHEW 1 : 20 - 23

20 But while he thought on these things, behold the angel of the LORD appeared unto him in a dream, saying, Joseph, thou son of David, fear not to take unto thee Mary thy wife: for that which is conceived in her is of the Holy Ghost.

21 And she shall bring forth a son, and thou shall call his name JESUS: for he shall save his people from their sins. Now as you can see that Joseph was familiar with the book of Isaiah which says

22 Now all this was done, that it might be fulfilled which was spoken of the LORD saying,

23 Behold a virgin shall be with child shall bring forth a son, and they shall call his name Emmanuel, which being interpreted is, GOD with us.

When he woke up from sleep Joseph did not query it, he did just what he was told of the angel. Do you think you would have done the same? If not, ask yourself why?

Food for thought: Do you believe in GOD so much that you can trust Him at His Word?

Shepherd's first told of the coming of Christ

Angels came to the shepherds to announce the birth of Christ. These shepherds were humble men but GOD chose these people amongst all others to celebrate with the angels the birth of His Son. They were the first to recognize a King that the rest of the world refused to acknowledge.

ST. LUKE 2 : 13 - 14

13 And suddenly there was with the angel a multitude of the heavenly host praising GOD, and saying,

14 Glory to GOD in the highest, and on earth peace, goodwill towards men.

GOD is no respecter of persons. He will use anyone for His Glory, so children of the Most

High stand firm in the liberty that you have been called into.

Angels rolled away the stone

ST. MATTHEW 28 : 1 - 8

1 In the end of the Sabbath, as it began to dawn towards the first day of the week, came Mary Magdalene and the other Mary to see the sepulchre.

2 And, behold, there was a great earthquake: for the angel of LORD descended from heaven, and came and rolled back the stone from the door, and sat upon it.

3 His countenance was like lightening, and his raiment white as snow:

4 And for fear of him the keepers did shake, and became as dead men.

5 And the angel answered and said unto the women, Fear not ye: for I know that he seek Jesus, which was crucified.

6 He is not here: for he is risen, as he said. Come, see the place where the LORD lay.

7 And go quickly, and tell his disciples that he is risen from the dead; and, behold, he goeth before you into Galilee; there shall ye see him: lo, I have told you.

8 And they departed quickly from the sepulchre with fear and great joy; and did run to bring his disciples word."

The angel came and rolled the stone away. Not only did he roll it away, he sat upon it. This event took place when Jesus–Yeshua Hamashiach had risen from the dead. Whatever, there be that represents that stone in your life, that is blocking your progress in life, pray that GOD will remove it from you completely and that the desires of your heart will be granted to you.

Angels tend to appear as dazzling light, wearing white apparel. Angels are created by GOD pure, like Adam our fore father was until he sinned.

Angels to give instruction

THE ACTS 10 : 1 – 8

1 “There was a certain man in Caesarea called Cornelius, a centurion of the band called the Italian band.

2 A devout man, and one that feared GOD with all his house, which gave much alms to the people, and prayed to GOD alway.

3 He saw in a vision evidently about the ninth hour of the day an angel of GOD coming in to him, and saying unto him, Cornelius.

4 And when he looked on him, he was afraid, and said, What is it, LORD? And he said unto him, Thy prayers and thine alms are come up for a memorial before GOD.

5 And now send men to Joppa, and call for one Simon, whose surname is Peter:

6 He lodgeth with one Simon a tanner, by the sea side: he shall tell thee what thou oughtest to do.

7 And when the angel which spake unto Cornelius was departed, he called two of his household servants, and a devout soldier of them that waited on him continually;

8 And when he had declared all these things unto them, he sent them to Joppa."

We find that an angel descended from heaven to a man named Cornelius who was a soldier and told him to send for Peter who was in Joppa. When Peter came he led Cornelius and his household to Salvation.

Definition of salvation: It means to salvage. When there is a shipwreck divers go down to see what can be saved. It means to save one from one's sins, to rescue or deliver from going to hell.

The LORD can save you from anything no matter what. If you hear and listen to Him. You must be aware that not every angel works for GOD.

Those angels that do not work for GOD are called demons and fallen angels.

These angels came in this time whether it was past or present. We see also in the vision of what is to come, John was the one who saw this. He was an Apostle of the LORD Jesus Christ.

In the bible The book of revelations talks of angels who minister consistently in heaven.

Satan Counterfeits GOD

We find that there are other archangels; they are Michael who is the warrior, Gabriel the messenger of joy, Raphael the healer, and Uriel the writer.

The Devil does everything just like GOD however, his own is not real - it is a counterfeit. There is only a thin line between the devil's works and GOD's, that is why one needs the spirit of wisdom and discernment.

Let me give you an everyday example. The man who does not know GOD and even sometimes those who do, will not wait upon GOD for an answer to their problems, but will make their way to mediums, fortune tellers, clairvoyance and such likes to get their problems solved.

Just like Saul the King of Israel, who had cut off witches and wizards throughout the land when he was obedient to GOD because GOD had said suffer not a witch to live, went against the will of GOD and sent his servants to find one to consult with.

When sin gets a hold of a person they have no control of their lives for evil manipulates them until GOD steps in. Praise GOD, He intervenes on time.

1 SAMUEL 28 : 7

7 Then Saul said, unto his servants, Seek me a woman that hath a familiar spirit, that I may go to her, and enquire of her, And his servants said to him, Behold, there is a woman that has a familiar spirit at En-dor.

Looking for a solution is going to GOD Almighty. GOD speaks through His Words and His prophets. Remember that a prophet is GOD's mouthpiece, so all one has to do is be patient.

My Testimony

Many years ago, when I was in my early Twenties (at the time of writing this I am now sixty two years old.) I was not happy with the children's father. This could have been avoided if only I had listened to GOD, who had sent a man of GOD – my Pastor – all the way to my home to speak with my mum and I, warning me not to marry this man.

But since I was hard ears and stubborn, I did my own thing. When things got too much for me, I am a person who likes to fast and pray. This is actually my second nature.

I opened my mouth and said to GOD, "if you don't give a solution by the morning I will be going to the fortune teller."

I suppose GOD was thinking what a wayward child. Okay dear, we will see who is the child and who is the Father, so I made my way the following day to a woman in Shepherd's Bush where I had grown up.

At that time I was living in Enfield. I had made my way the previous evening to my friend's house and had asked her to look after the children for a few hours for me. She was living in Harlesden, where she resides to this day. I went to the fortune teller and after seeing her, collected my children and went back home.

Clearly as you can see, my mind was already made up to see the fortune teller. Otherwise, I would not have left my home to go to my friend's house with an agenda. GOD just left me to my devices. I did not go to church, I stayed at home. About two weeks later I went to church with my children's father who was a Sunday School Superintendent in the church we both attended. It was the same church but a different branch in which my Pastor had come to my home. The church was having a programme and he was doing something so he wanted me to attend. He went as far as to get me a very nice coat so I would go along with him.

Oh my days, GOD loves me so much that He made sure I went. He was getting ready to take me out of this world unless I repent of going to the fortune teller, but He wanted to give me another chance.

That night was a Holy Ghost night. The preacher preached just to me. The pastor's wife came and led me to the altar.

I remember my son's Godfather was playing the guitar right in front of me so I had to speak quietly. The Pastor who was doing the altar call began to speak with me when I was telling GOD I was sorry, he answered saying 'you sorry, you sorry, you sorry, You are to lift me up why did you go to the witch? Why did you knock on her door?' I answered because of what was happening to me. He said David said I will look unto the hills from whence cometh my help, you should have come to me.

We kept talking back and forth. I said sorry again. He went into one and let me know plain and straight, no beating about the bush. He said your heart is evil, get under blood, ask me to forgive you.This went on and on. GOD was tarrying with me through the Pastor. When I got up from the altar he was too far to have heard me.

I had been whispering so quietly that not even my son's Godfather could hear my words, despite being within arm's reach. Thus the Man of GOD, who was further away could not have heard my prayers.

On the way home I found why the pastor had stopped so abruptly as I said GOD was tarrying through him for me. I understand that he had gone way overtime and had to be stopped.

I went home and began in earnest to fast and pray and ask Papa not to take me out and that I would lift him up. It seems that no one could understand why the man of GOD spoke so long. After a few weeks I owned up that he was talking to me.

So those of you who have churches and will have one, ask GOD for your own building so that when GOD wants to save a soul He can do so with ease.

If He just wants His People to be with Him all night, it is possible. I can tell you GOD is real and He goes out of His way for the one that goes astray.

ST. LUKE 19 : 10

10 For the son of man is come to seek and to save that which was lost.

ST. MATTHEW 18 : 12 - 14

12 How think ye? If a man have an hundred sheep, and one of them be gone astray, doth he not leave the ninety and nine, and goeth into the mountains, and seeketh that which is gone astray?

13 And if so be that he find it, verily I say unto you, he rejoiceth more of that sheep, than the ninety and nine which went not astray.

14 Even so it is not the will of your Father which is in heaven, that one of these little one should perish.

We humans need to show compassion when dealing with those who err, because but for the grace of GOD it could have been any one of us.

One of my favourite songs

There was ninety and nine that was safely lay

In the shelter of the fold,

But one was out on the hills away,

Far off from the gates of gold;

Away on the mountains wild and bare,

Away from the tender Shepherd's care.

2 "LORD, Thou hast here Thy ninety and nine,

Are they not enough for thee ?"

But the Shepherd made answer:

"This of Mine Has wandered away from Me;

And, although the road be rough and steep,

I go to the desert to find My sheep."

3 But none of the ransomed ever knew

How deep were the waters cross'd;

Nor how dark was the night that the

LORD pass'd through,

Ere He found His sheep that was lost,

Out in the dessert He heard its cry-

Sick, and helpless, and ready to die.

4 " LORD, whence are those blood drops all the way,

That mark out the mountain's track?"

"They were shed for one who had gone astray

Ere the Shepherd could bring him back."

"LORD whence are thy hands so rent and torn ?"

"They are pierced to- night by many a thorn"

5 But all through the mountains thunder- riven,

And up from the rocky steep,

There arose a cry to the gates of heaven:

"Rejoice ! I have found My sheep!"

And the angels echoed around the throne,

"Rejoice! for the LORD brings back His own!"

If you read these words, pray and meditate on them, you may experience a change in your emotional state. Let the words reach beyond emotions and touch your very soul for the lives of men, women, boys and girls around the world, especially in your families and communities are fundamental.

GOD is counting on us. Will you go and help the Master in bringing back His Own? Will you make an effort to do so? Remember He is with you and He will work with you confirming His words with signs following.

The Angel of the LORD opens up prison doors

THE ACTS 5 : 17 - 20

17 Then the high priest rose up, and all they that were with him, (which is the sect of the Sadducees,) and were filled with indignation,

18 And laid their hands on the apostles, and put them in the common prison,

19 But the angel the of LORD by night opened the prison doors, and brought them forth, and said,

20 Go, stand and speak in the temple to the people all the words of this life.

Here you see where the Apostles were put in prison for preaching the word of GOD; I believe this was our LORD. The Apostles had not gone to prison before although He had warned them prior that it was a possibility. He told them to go to the temple to speak to the people and He had reassured His Apostles that they are never alone.

Likewise we must know that He will make a way for us when there is no way. The gates of hell cannot stop the calling that GOD has for His chosen people and we need to be bold to tell the people of His love. That is what He expects us to do.

Phillip commissioned by the angel of the LORD

THE ACTS 8 : 26

26 And the angel of the LORD spake unto Phillip, saying, Arise, and go towards the south unto the way that goeth down from Jerusalem unto Gaza which is desert.

We see that the GOD we serve is ever faithful, He had promised and He continues to deliver so let nothing deter you from doing the work of the Messiah. As we keep seeing from Scripture, all that the GODhead wants is that people should not be lost to sin and hell but to have everlasting life.

When Phillip obeyed and went and witnessed the eunuch, that man was converted and was baptised.

He did not keep it to himself, he went to his country and brought others into the kingdom.

It is worth noting that the famous Evangelist Billy Graham was the only person that turned up at the revival. He gave his life to Christ and look today at the majority of souls that he has brought, I am sure that though that Man of GOD who had put on that programme might have been disappointed then. Later on when he realized what GOD had done through him I believe he rejoiced.

I would like you to ponder over this and know that the LORD Jesus is counting on us. He has made us to be fishers of men.

ST. MATTHEW 4 : 19

19 And he saith unto them, Follow me, and I will make you fishers of men.

Let us fulfil that great commission of winning souls of men for the Master. There are so many people who are dying without Christ. Would you believe that some have never heard of Him? It is time to make a difference. Glory to GOD.

The Angel of the LORD stands by His people

As the gospel began to spread, the powers of darkness were not happy about it so they used the king whose name was Herod to vex the church. He killed James, the brother of John.

Now the Jews they were very happy about this. Given that this pleased them, Herod decided to take Peter as well, putting him in prison until after Easter to bring him to the people. However, the Angel of the LORD intervened once again and delivered Peter. It was done so perfectly that Peter thought he was having a vision.

THE ACTS 12 : 7 – 10

7 And, behold, the angel of the LORD came upon
him, and a light shined in the prison: and he smote

Peter on the side, and raised him up, saying, Arise
up quickly. And his chains fell off from his hands.

8 And the angel said unto him, Gird thyself, and
bind on thy sandals. And so he did. And he saith
unto him, Cast thy garment about thee, and follow
me.

9 And he went out, and followed him; and wist
not that it was true which was done by the angel;
but thought he saw a vision.

10 When they were past the first and the second
ward, they came unto the iron gate that leadeth
unto the city; which opened to them of his own
accord: and they went out, and passed on through
one street; and forthwith the angel departed from
him.

Children of GOD know that when you walk with GOD, gates that have been closed to you in order to hinder your destiny will open for you of their own accord. No gate and no door can remain closed when Jesus shows up on your behalf.

Prayer

ISAIAH 45 : 2

2 I will go before thee, and make the crooked places straight: I will break in pieces the gates of brass, and cut in sunder the bars of iron.

1 Pray that every chain that the enemy has placed upon you be removed and be completely destroyed.
2 Father in the name of Jesus let every gate of brass be removed and destroyed this day and forever more.
3 Jesus you are LORD of my life, every bar of iron cut them asunder and destroy them and I will give you all the glory.
4 Almighty GOD please make every crooked path in my life straight.
5 Father I give you thanks, I love and adore you. You are mighty to save. Amen.

The Angel of the LORD to give judgement

You will see that we don't have to worry about who is doing this or that just make sure you are living right. Children of GOD we have a righteous Judge. There is nothing that occurs that His eyes do not see or that He is not aware of. So leave everything in His care and let Him do Justice.

Look at Balaam, the man of GOD was told 'no' by GOD but still he wanted to go with Balak because of money. When the money increased, instead of saying no he decided he was going back to GOD again and asked if he could go.

I wonder which part of what GOD said he did not understand. When finally GOD said Yes, even His donkey by the Supernatural power of GOD spoke and this Man of GOD was so busy answering the donkey that he did not realize that donkeys do not talk.

Don't let us be so blinded by sin that we do not see what the LORD is trying to reveal to us. Let us be in tune with Him at all times not just to hear but also listen to what He is telling us to do.

The Angel of the LORD Himself descended to give Judgement. If it had not been for Balaam's donkey he would have been a goner. The donkey had to save his master's life three times during the journey when the Angel of the LORD stood in the way with a sword drawn as He did in Jerusalem when David had disobeyed Him.

NUMBERS 22 : 32

32 And the angel of the LORD said unto him, Wherefore hast thou smitten thine ass these three

times? behold, I went out to withstand thee, because thy way is preserve before me.

Let us not give our Saviour unnecessary provocation.

1ST CHRONICLES 21 : 16

16 And David lifted up his eyes, and saw the angel of the LORD stand between the earth and the heaven, having a drawn sword in his hand stretched out over Jerusalem. Then David and the elders of Israel, who were clothed in sackcloth, fell upon their faces.

Also in Jerusalem during the time of king Hezekiah when the king of Assyria caused his people to invade Judea and caused his man Rabshaketh to go to Jerusalem to do the same, GOD intervened.

ISAIAH 37 : 36

36 Then the angel of the LORD went forth, and smote in camp of the Assyians a hundred and fourscore and five thousand.

Christians do not know how powerful their GOD is. He will fight for you Himself if need be. He will not let your enemies laugh at you. However, should they do so, this is not a problem. They think they are doing you a disservice but this is not so, the disservice is to GOD.

PSALM 54 : 7

7 For he hath delivered me out of all trouble: and mine eyes hath seen his desire upon my enemies.

Remember it is not about you but Him.

THE ACTS 33 : 21 – 23

21 And upon a set day Herod, arrayed in royal apparel, sat upon his throne, and made an oration unto them.

22 And the people gave a shout, saying, It is the voice of a GOD, and not a man.

23 And immediately the angel of the LORD smote him, because he gave not GOD the glory: and he was eaten of worms, and gave up the ghost.

Here you find the angel of the LORD in His might as a Judge. No other can judge like Him for He is a Righteous Judge. 'He will not give His Glory to another.'

Let us always remember to give GOD the Glory so we do not fall into the same predicament as Herod the King who the Angel of the LORD slew for his **blasphemy**.

This warning is especially important for you men and women of GOD. Please don't let people make you fall by sweet-talking you, till you forget that you are not your own, that you belong to the most High GOD.

PSALMS 62 : 11

11 GOD has spoken once; twice have I heard this; that power belongeth unto GOD.

You must immediately point these people to GOD, letting them know that all **power** belongs to Him and that you are just on business for the King so that we all make it in. Praise GOD, Hallelujah, Glory, Glory, Glory to His matchless name! The name above every other name. The name of Jesus is the sweetest name in all the earth. Let us bless His holy name.

Worship LORD GOD

Praise Him from out of your belly that out of it will flow rivers of Living Water that will gust forth to affect lives and change them for the Master.

Angels reassure us

THE ACTS 27 : 23 – 24

23 For there stood by me this night the angel of the GOD, whose I am, and whom I serve,

24 Saying, Fear not, Paul; thou must be brought before Caesar: and, lo, GOD hath given thee all them that sail with thee.

Paul was on his journey to Rome for when he went to Jerusalem they had apprehended him. He appealed to be heard by Caesar though he was not guilty of what was said of him.

Now, there are times in a person's life they will do or say something thinking that is what they want not knowing you are walking in your destiny so it is very important that we always ask the LORD to guide us day and night and to direct our paths.

During the voyage to Rome the ship that they were in had to stop at a place called the haven. Here Paul had told the centurion and the owner of the ship that he foresaw damage occurring to the ship as it looked like a storm was coming. They did not listen to him and carried on their journey as the haven was not that safe for them to stay there. They were hoping to go to a safer place and when the southwind blew gently, they thought it was good for them to go ahead.

On their way came a storm! They had to throw things overboard to lighten the ship and the storm was so strong there was neither sun or stars. They also did not eat any food for fourteen days and, as the storm was very great, all hope of survival had left them.

The angel of The LORD made His appearance, to reassure Paul that he would not lose his life and that those who sailed with him would live. If we ever give up hope, GOD will always intervene to reassure us.

Paul told these men all that the LORD had told him and he said all came to pass. Probably because Paul was on board the ship no person lost their life. GOD said He allows the sun to shine on the just and unjust alike.

Even though the haven was not safe to stay, if they had obeyed Paul no harm would have come to them. When we are told by GOD to do something that might not seem right, we should obey once we are certain that it is GOD.

PSALM 91 : 1

1 He that dwelleth in the secret place of the most High shall abide under the shadow of the Almighty.

Children of GOD abide in Him for if we do, no harm can befall us nor will any danger come nigh us.

Many angels can come to a person at a time

Take Moses for example, to whom ten thousands of angels appeared when he was on the mount of Sinai.

DEUTERONOMY 33 : 2

2 And he said, The LORD came from Sinai, and rose up from Seir unto them; he shined forth from mount Paran, and he came with ten thousands of saints; from his right hand went a fiery law for them.

David saw twenty thousand chariots and thousands of angels.

PSALM 68 : 17

17 The chariots of GOD are twenty thousand,
even thousands of angels: the LORD is among
them, as in Sinai, in the holy place.

Angels are organised

In the Scriptures we read where Jesus could have called twelve legions of angels to fight on His behalf if He wanted to but, because of the Assignment on His life to save mankind He did not do this.

ST. MATTHEW 26 : 53

53 Thinkest thou that I cannot now pray to my Father, and he shall presently give me more than twelve legions of angels?

There are so many angels in heaven and we can assume they are more than the world populations. So those elders and scribes that came that night to take our Saviour would not have stood a chance if He had prayed to His Father our GOD to send help.

Also let us remember that the angel's foremost occupation (work) is to protect us. When we are in danger of any kind, let us call out to Jesus and ask Him to send His angels to minister on our behalf and He will.

Angels will gather the elect

ST. MATTHEW 24 : 31

31 And he shall send his angels with a great sound of a trumpet and, they shall gather together his elect from the four winds, from one end of heaven to the other.

This Scripture tells us what will happen in the end, when He comes the second time. His first coming was recorded for us in the Gospels according to ST. MATTHEW, ST. MARK and ST. LUKE. He came unto His own and His own received Him not but we know that Jesus – Yeshua Hamashiach, He Himself will descend and send His Angels to gather up His people. Glory be to GOD.

Amen.

CONCLUSION

There are so many angels GOD has created to be superior to us and they are around us on earth, as well as in heaven. These angels are employed in the service of GOD. Later on when we are changed and have become immortal beings we shall be higher than them for the Bible states that we shall judge angels. We find throughout scriptures that when it was not our LORD and Saviour ministering in the form of the angel of the LORD or GOD you find archangels and other angels doing so.

Each protecting, guiding, instructing and delivering GOD'S people. In the future you see that angels will play an active role. One thing you must realise is that angels do not take worship. There is only one angel who receives worship in scripture and that is the angel of the LORD for He is GOD.

JOSHUA 5 : 14 – 15

14 And he said, Nay; but as captain of the host of the LORD am I now come. And Joshua fell on his face to the earth, and did worship, and said unto him, What saith my LORD unto his servant?

15 And the captain of the LORD'S host said unto Joshua, Loose thy shoe from off thy foot; for the place whereon thou standest is holy. And Joshua did so.

Unlike the angel who revealed the end times to John in the book of Revelation.

REVELATION 19 : 10

10 And I fell at his feet to worship him. And he said unto me, See thou do it not: I am thy fellow servant, and of thy brethren that have the testimony of Jesus: worship GOD.

REVELATIONS 22 : 8 - 9

8 And I John saw these things, and heard them. And when I had heard and seen, I fell down to worship before the feet of the angel which shewed me these things.

9 Then saith he unto me, See thou do it not: for I am thy fellow servant and of thy brethren the prophets, and of them which keep the sayings of this book: worship GOD.

Angels do not want or receive worship. Why do men seek this when they are not GOD? May GOD have mercy on our souls and keep us from falling. Amen.

JUDE 24 - 25

24 Now unto him that is able to keep you from falling, and to present you faultless before the presence of his glory with exceeding joy,

25 To the only wise GOD our Saviour, be glory majesty, dominion and power, both now and ever. Amen.

I pray the will of GOD in these words over your life - AMEN.

OTHER BOOKS BY MARIE LAKE

The Angel Of The Lord

Women Of Power

www.ingramcontent.com/pod-product-compliance
Lightning Source LLC
LaVergne TN
LVHW050556160826
845677LV00011B/2334

* 9 7 9 8 5 4 9 4 1 3 9 0 0 *